FULFILLING DREAMS

THE JOURNEY OF A YOUNG COUPLE WHO MOVED TO PORT PROTECTION, ALASKA TO FOLLOW THEIR DREAMS

Patty Mae Gray

Acknowledgments

I want to thank the special individuals in the community of Port Protection, Alaska for sharing their wonderful recipes with me. You can substitute any item in any meal plan with what you have available; feel free to be creative. When you live in a remote village, you learn to cook with what you have. I would also like to dedicate this book to the readers who entrenched themselves in my journey.

The order of my recipes I dedicate to my mother, Babe Webb, for all the meals she served to our family of eight, our neighborhood friends, and my father's fishing buddies.

To my father, Art Webb, for teaching me about the love of fishing.
I have lost both my parents to cancer.

CONTENTS

INTRODUCTION

I chose to write this book after moving from Washington to Port Protection, Alaska to start a full-service fishing lodge. I had been asked several times by lodge guests, "What made you sell everything and move to Port Protection, Alaska to start a fishing lodge?" The other question asked most often was about our recipes. This made me feel so proud. I had thought we would be able to hire a cook but realized we couldn't afford it at the time. I had to do the cooking. I lost sleep. I had to work so hard to find the easiest and best recipes and put a meal plan together, including lunches for our guests to eat on the boats. I kept a journal that I am now sharing.

CHAPTER I

CHILDHOOD MEMORIES

Our home in Ballard, Washington was always the meeting destination for my father and his friends to meet prior to hunting or fishing.

My mother always had a large pot of clam chowder, chili, stew, or spaghetti on the stove for not only our family of eight children but also for all our friends. Our friends would always rave about how good of a cook my mom was. Mom became popular in the neighborhood because of her meals. She always made large lunches for my father's fishing trips, which often included carrot cake.

My father enjoyed the art of smoking the fish, and he was the best at it. We followed his recipe at the lodge.

My brother, an avid fisherman, requested we add a seafood fettuccine to our menu as well as good wine. My brother and I were on the deck of the lodge, enjoying the bay view. He made the comment that if my dad were still here, he would be very proud of what we had built. That meant a lot to me to hear that.

Tom and I were both born and raised in Seattle, Washington. We both enjoyed fishing and the outdoors. Prior to moving to Port Protection, Alaska, we lived in Snohomish, Washington at the mouth of the Skykomish River.

Tom and I met while fishing at the Ballard Locks in Seattle, Washington. I was going through a divorce. I would go fishing by myself on the local lakes. I used to love to go out and explore new fishing areas by myself. I would put my trolling motor in the back of my Toyota truck with my fiberglass boat, fishing poles, and tackle box. Then, when I found a lake, I would use that battery out of my truck to run the motor. It was fine as long as the wind didn't blow too hard—but when it did, it would get a little scary.

This time, I thought I would go to Ballard Locks. Tom saw me; he fished there often with his friends. When Tom was a kid, he would sell the fish he caught to his teachers and neighbors. He asked if he could help me fish. I told him I had it figured out even though I didn't. As it turned out, both of us went to the China Chef, a local bar that played a two-man band. Tom asked me to dance after noticing I wasn't wearing a wedding ring anymore, then asked for my phone number. He called to see if I would like to go steelhead fishing, which would soon be our first date. I agreed, but I was hesitant since I was just going through a divorce. I really didn't like Tom, nor was I attracted to him.

"You need to get to know him," a friend said. "He is a nice guy."

Once I got to know him, his personality won me over. He was a real gentleman and made me laugh. I was at home when Tom called to see if he could come by to visit. I told him I was sick. I didn't feel like having company. A while later, my doorbell rang, but I didn't answer. When I thought he was gone, I looked outside and found flowers and a card from Tom.

I stood Tom up on the first steelhead fishing date we were supposed to go on. He was not going to give me another chance, but I talked him into it. "I won't do it again," I promised him.

It was a fun time. I was very nervous. We went to the Skykomish River. I was excited to cast my line somewhere I hadn't fished before. There were a couple of other guys fishing. I caught the biggest buck steelhead I had ever seen. It was exciting having the guys watch me pull the big fish in. I was hooked.

I prayed to God to help me find someone who would make me laugh, someone to love—a best friend. After spending time with Tom, I realized he was the opposite of my ex-husband. My prayers were answered with Tom.

After dating for a while, I was having issues with my ex-husband threatening me at work. I was very frightened by him.

Tom asked me to come to Alaska to fish with him on his commercial fishing boat. I thought he was kidding. He wasn't. I also knew I needed to get away from my abusive ex-husband. I had dated Tom long enough to feel safe going with him. I quit my job, sold my furniture, and went commercial fishing with Tom.

I did not enjoy being a deckhand. It was all business. I was now his employee. I was excited about a new adventure but scared because I really didn't know what I was getting myself into. Cleaning fish holds, picking fish out of the net, and getting up at all times of the night. Tom did let me sleep in occasionally. One day, he slowed the boat down to a drift. He made a fabulous turkey dinner on the boat in the middle of the bay with porpoises swimming around the boat. It was very romantic.

On Saturdays, we would have date night on the boat. Tom would pull into a cove to anchor for the night. We would have a nice dinner, then end up in the bunk for a romantic night. I ended up getting pregnant. I was afraid to tell Tom. I finally summoned the courage.

"What are we going to do?" he asked, completely surprised.

"I am keeping it with or without your support," I said.

"Will I still be able to fish?" he asked.

"Will you still bring me flowers?" I asked.

We both agreed. After about a month, I started having cramps. When I called my mother, she told me to come home. I needed to see a doctor, so I had to go back to Washington.

When I got to Washington, my father was taking my aunt and uncle back to Montana after my uncle had cancer treatment in Seattle. Dad asked if I wanted to go with them. I had to find out about the cramping first. I saw the nurse practitioner. She said the baby was making room. It was okay. So, I went with Dad.

When we got to Montana, I was shopping with my aunt, and I got bad cramps. I knew something wasn't right. I was sweating badly and felt hungry. "We have to go," I told my aunt.

When we got to the house, I thought I needed to eat something. I took a bite out of an apple. The pain just got worse. "I have to go to the emergency room," I told my dad.

At the hospital, I found out I had a tubular pregnancy that burst. It was devastating. I think it was the first time I had seen my dad cry. He blamed himself for asking me to go with him to Montana.

After we were married in October 1992, I would get depressed when it was time for Tom to go to Alaska for six months as a commercial fisherman. He always seemed so excited. It was as though he was happy to leave me behind. Those were my thoughts. He was just busy with all that he had to do before he left. It became harder for both of us.

I was busy selling real estate in Snohomish, Washington. This would help when Tom was home in the winter. It was also slow for real estate. This gave us more time to spend together when Tom was home.

In the fall and winter, when Tom was home from commercial fishing, he averaged six days a week steelhead fishing in Washington. Fishing was Tom's life; he had been doing it in Alaska commercially for 18 years.

Tom had come home two years in a row telling me about these lodges he had looked at, and for the past two years, he wasn't as excited about commercial fishing. Tom was ready for a change. I figured I could do whatever I set my mind to do. When Tom and I talked about owning and operating a fishing lodge, we said if the right property became available and the price and terms were at our comfort level, we would do it. So many times, you hear, "I wish I would have done this or that."

We figured at least we could say, "We did it."

CHAPTER 2

CONSIDERING MAKING THE MOVE

When Tom was in Alaska fishing, he called me to tell me about a lodge he was thinking of looking at. We had fished this area when I was with him, so I knew how beautiful it was. But the price was way more than we could afford. At the time, we hadn't seriously decided whether to buy a property for a lodge or not. I started a green goods business. I told Tom before I invested any more in the green goods business I needed to know if he was serious about the lodge business. "Is this something you think you can enjoy doing?" I asked.

"It doesn't hurt to look," he replied.

I had inherited some property from my aunt and uncle in Montana who ran a resort there. I always wanted to reinvest the money into another waterfront property.

A couple of weeks after Tom looked at the first lodge, he saw an ad on a property that he had called about a year before. The building was only a frame at that time. The agent told him the house on the property was more complete but still needed some work.

Tom called me to tell me about the property. He said Anita, the seller, lived in a beach house next to the dock on the waterfront property. Anita made Tom cookies on an old wood-burning stove. The lodge was up the hill from the beach house. He said it could work for what we would like to do. Anita was an elderly lady. She and her husband started to build the lodge. They had dreams of running the lodge, until her husband had a heart attack on the beach. Anita lost her husband and their dreams. Her son completed the lodge to the state it was currently in. The lodge was constructed of red and yellow cedar milled on the beach next to the beach house.

I had so many emotions going on. Excited, nervous, and sad to be moving away from family.

We decided it was all or nothing. We negotiated a price and terms that would work for us. Anita accepted our offer.

The property would give us a way of building sweat equity into it in case the business didn't succeed. We wanted to make sure we would be able to make a profit. I always try to look at worst-case scenarios.

We sold our home in Snohomish and started our journey to Alaska.

We closed on the sale of the property in October 1994. We loaded a 40-foot container with all our furniture, carpets for the lodge, eight beds, four dressers, an armoire, and a China hutch. The container would go on a barge to ship to Port Protection. We loaded our clothes, our cat Sockeye, and our dog Coho into our truck, then drove for six days to get to our new home in Port Protection.

Port Protection, a community of approximately 70 people, is a beautiful, sheltered inlet. This small community is known to be one of the richest fishing areas in Alaska. You can see whales, black bears, seals, eagles, deer, and seabirds. The wildlife scenery provides wonderful opportunities for photography and for adventures. Of course, there is always fishing. There are no roads to the village. The only access is by boat or float plane. Port Protection is located on Prince of Wales Island, the third largest island in the United States. There is a road system on the island; a logging road.

Human remains from 9,800 years ago were found in a cave near Port Protection, as well as 30,000-year-old brown bear and caribou remains. Archeologists figure this was a hunting camp used for many years long ago. These human remains are the oldest found on the North American coast.

CHAPTER 3

THE JOURNEY TO PORT PROTECTION

O ur journey began on October 28th, 1994. We left Snohomish, Washington in our Ford F-350 with our dog Coho and cat Sockeye at approximately 3:30 p.m. and arrived in Burlington, Washington at 4:35 p.m. We stayed at my in-laws for the night to get an early start the next morning. We left Burlington on October 29th, 1994, at 9:30 a.m. We stopped in Ferndale to see my sister and look at a couple of furniture stores. We were going to need more furniture for the lodge. We left Ferndale at 1:15 p.m.

We went through Spences Bridge, a community in the Canadian province of British Columbia. Spences Bridge is 164.5 miles north of the Blaine, Washington border. You have to look out for mountain sheep on the road. They were in yards and on the side of the road. People were stopping to take pictures.

We arrived in Cashe Creek at 6 p.m. We stayed the night at the Desert Motel. It was a small, tranquil motel. We had a hot breakfast at the

Chum restaurant around the corner from the motel. We left Cashe Creek at 9 a.m.

We started to study to get our Alaska State driver's license as soon as we reached Ketchikan. I would read out loud to Tom while he drove. We tested each other when we got to the hotel.

Just outside of Clinton, we ran into snow. Tom had to put the truck into four-wheel drive. I was a little scared, not knowing how much snow we would run into. We continued our journey to Port Protection. There wasn't a lot of snow once we got to the 70-mile house. It was clear and beautiful. We arrived in Vanderhoof, British Columbia at 5 p.m. and stayed the night. We got up early the next morning. It was snowing, and the ground was covered. We had breakfast at Grandma's Café and were on the road again at 7 a.m. The scenic drive from Telkwa, British Columbia, with the Bulkley and Skeena Rivers and Seven Sister Mountains, was gorgeous. We left the snow just past Topley. The rest of the trip to Prince Rupert had the most rivers and mountains I had ever seen.

We noticed all along the way that there were garbage barrels to eliminate littering, which must have worked because the highway was pretty much litter-free.

We arrived in Prince Rupert at approximately 3:30 p.m. We stayed the night and checked into the ferry terminal at 6:30 a.m. The ferry was scheduled to depart at 8:30 a.m. We arrived in Ketchikan, Alaska at 1:30 p.m. It was a beautiful ferry ride. We both took the state exam to get our Alaska driver's licenses; we both passed and received them on the spot. We then stopped to register to vote. We stayed the night in Ketchikan.

In the morning, we caught the ferry to Hollis, Alaska, located on Prince of Wales Island. We arrived in Hollis at 10:30 a.m. We then drove to Craig and Klawock, Alaska.

Klawock only had one lodge that was full. So, we went to Craig, where we arrived at 1:15 p.m. We had dinner at Ruth Ann's restaurant. The food was excellent, with fresh seafood, steak, and home-cooked meals.

We stayed the night at the Hideaway Lodge. This was the only hotel or lodge that would not allow our pets to stay. Coho and Sockeye had to spend the night in the truck. Sockeye was in the Vari kennel with bedding and her cat box. She was comfortable. Coho had carpet to lay on, so he was comfortable also. It wasn't too cold for them either.

Wednesday, we got up at 5:00 a.m. and went shopping for groceries. It was going to be a four-hour drive on logging roads to the end of the road, where David, a member of the Port Protection community, met us with a skiff to take us for a 15-minute ride to the property.

Tom and David dropped me, Coho, and Sockeye off with as much stuff as we were able to fit in the skiff. They went back for the rest of our stuff.

The lodge was cold. The fireplace hadn't been going for a long time. We were exhausted physically and mentally, so we went to bed early.

There was a lot of cleaning up to do. The beach house needed cosmetic work. The lodge only needed carpets and a vapor barrier... or so we thought.

Our furniture was coming the following day in a 40-foot container.

We had a few village people willing to help in any way they could to unload the container.

CHAPTER 4

FURNITURE ARRIVES

On November 5th, our container arrived at 9:30 a.m. The people in the community were wonderful. We had 10 to 12 people to help us unload. They all started unloading the container with no complaints. I directed everyone to where to put the items. They all made us feel welcome. We finished unloading at 1:30 p.m. I made grilled cheese sandwiches for everyone, and Tom bought beer.

We were able to visit with everyone for a while when we finished unloading.

On November 18th, 1994, we were using Tom's little generator to power lights. We had a propane stove to cook on until we could get the neighbor to help Tom rewire the electrical panel in the house and get the big generator running.

We had been keeping food cold in the ice chests and taking frozen food over to the trading post to keep in the freezer there.

We only had one channel on the TV, the Alaskan channel. We really appreciated a good show when we could get it.

CHAPTER 5

WINTER SETS IN

W e had about two inches of snow on the ground for several days. Last night it rained. There was a boardwalk that went from the beach house to the lodge. It got slick. I fell at least four times—and that was without the snow. Tom decided to put tar paper down once the weather let up.

We had our carpets laid last week. What a difference it made. The space was much warmer and looked a lot better. The carpet layer had to stay an extra day because the float plane didn't come in on Sunday to pick him up due to the weather.

There were a few things we still needed to finish up at the lodge. The sliding doors were not installed properly. We had a Paloma water heater and an on-demand heater that was supposed to be used in a small house or single bathroom. We ordered a larger one, as well as heaters for all the rooms. Our only heat at the time was from the fireplace.

Our neighbor gave us some smoked salmon. One of the boat liveaboards gave us some Smelt, which was such a nice gesture. They call these neighbors "liveaboard" because they live on their boats and would tie up to the dock at the trading post.

Tom went over to the road system with a neighbor he met to get some firewood.

I stayed home and worked at the beach house.

I also finished our brochure for the lodge, except I needed good pictures to help market the place.

We went to our first water association meeting. We were now aware of people against any development, especially commercial businesses. But the majority were for growth. One lady commented that they didn't move to Port Protection to have big lodges move in around them. I knew it was important to let them know what to expect. It is the unknown that scares people. We let them know we planned on staying small.

CHAPTER 6

TRIP TO TOWN IN THE BOAT

Our neighbor went to one of the islands and shot four deer. We were given a couple of fresh deer steaks that we had for dinner that same night. It was a pretty good steak, but it needed a little more flavor. I hadn't had fresh deer meat in years. Our neighbors preserved their meat due to a lack of freezer space.

We also tried some canned turkey. It was good and inspired us to start canning as well.

It was so different living in the bush. You have to work for heat, food, and lights. You don't just turn on the switch. You have to make sure there is fuel in the generator. You have to hunt for wood in the skiff out in the ocean, bring it to the beach, cut it all up, and bring it up the hill to the lodge in the ATV, so you can start the fire, so you can have heat. You fish and hunt for your meat. Gardens are difficult in Alaska. There is not enough light and it's cold. Soil is like gold—it is hard to get. It is best to grow cool-weather crops. There are Huckleberries and blueberries around to pick.

We decided to try and get to town, only this time we were going to Petersburg in the boat. The wind was supposed to blow around 25 mph. I told Tom I trusted his judgment. "You're the captain," I said.

We had a rough time. Coho and I were feeling sick to our stomach, and I hadn't been so scared in all my life. We had water coming over the boat and it got dark by the time we even got close to our anchor spot. I couldn't see if there were any logs. All I could think was, "We will get through this. Tom will get us out of this."

Occasionally, I would look over at Tom to see if he seemed worried, and I would tell him I was afraid. He would tell me it was alright, and that would make me feel a little better. Eventually, Tom got us into the anchor spot safely. I was so relieved that I started to cry.

This trip to Petersburg was nothing like that, but I was still concerned. We had high waves that sent the boat sideways, making it feel like we were getting swallowed up in a washing machine. Tom slowed the boat down and I steered as he put the stabilizer out; that helped. Once we were through all that, Coho and I started feeling better. A sense of calmness washed over me. I kept red licorice and pretzels with us to help us feel better. I am not sure why licorice and pretzels helped, but they di.

Once in Petersburg, we did our Thanksgiving shopping and all our other shopping that needed to be done. They had six inches of snow during the time we were there. We stayed two days to get everything done.

The boat ride back home was beautiful; not rough at all.

For Thanksgiving, we invited David, Charlie, Maren, and Steven over for dinner. David brought the wine, Charlie and Maren brought pie. We had a feast.

David was a character. He moved to rural Alaska from New York to get away from drugs. He was a cab driver in New York and had some good stories to tell. He lived on a boat that he tied up at the trading post. He was a liveaboard neighbor. Once in the U.S. Army, he now had something like 30 guns, and he was a hoarder. He worked in a specialized trade. We fed him whenever he helped us out, and we would pay him.

There was a community water system at the end of a long boardwalk. There was a small rustic schoolhouse about halfway for the local kids to attend. Coho and I would walk up to the water tank every day to get out of the lodge and take a break before our nap. I had to regroup before the guests came back from fishing. Then we would start dinner and the evening routine. Most of the neighbors lived around the bay. Some lived up the boardwalk. We had other neighbors who lived in the back bay, located around the corner from our bay. You had to take a boat.

CHAPTER 7

FREEZING TEMPERATURES

November 30th, 1994. Tom and I were woken up at 5 a.m. by the wind. I got up to use the bathroom, and when I flushed the toilet, I noticed the water wasn't running. The wind froze the pipes. Tom got dressed and went under the house with the propane torch. We had a wood stove under the house that he started. At 6:55 a.m., we still didn't have water; daylight would be upon us soon. The wind had died down, so that could help. I had been trying to keep things warm inside with just the fireplace. I separated the rooms off with blankets. We stayed around the fireplace.

At 9:30 a.m., I started to make breakfast, and the water in the kitchen started to run. We had made progress. By 10:30 a.m., all the faucets and toilets were running again.

Tom had been cutting wood all week to get us caught up for a month or so. Then, he could take on other tasks that needed to be done. They had to take the skiff and a barge made from an old boat over to the end of the road system. They were allowed to cut dead trees off the state land and retrieved some nice burning wood. I had been staying home to keep the fire going and stay up to date on paperwork and anything else that needed to be done. This week, I had swollen glands and a slight cold. Even feeling sick, I got a lot done.

CHAPTER 8

MAKING PROGRESS

March 14ᵗʰ, 1995

We had been busy getting the lodge finished and restoring the beach house so we could move into the beach house by April 1ˢᵗ.

We finally got our brochures out and began advertising. We had a few calls from prospective clients but no other bookings from advertising just yet. Tom needed to install a new water heater at the lodge. The current one could only be used for a single faucet, and only one person at a time could use the hot water. Thankfully, he completed the electrical work in the lodge and hooked up the inverter, which was great. We shut off the generator at night, and the inverter would kick in so we could have lights at night whenever we needed them—a big accomplishment. We still needed to replace the windows in two of the rooms because they wouldn't open.

There were a few other small items that needed to be done, and the lodge would be finished. We hadn't decided how to set up the solarium. We knew we wanted a gift shop and plants but needed to work on that. That was my last priority.

I had been working at the beach house. I finished painting today. I tore out some walls and shelves to replace them with others—there were shelves every-where.

When not working at the beach house, I was working on the menu. I lost a lot of sleep over the meal planning. I never had to plan meals before. Now, I had to plan dinners, lunch, breakfast, snacks, and appetizers.

When Tom and I were first married, I had a hard time with my cooking. No matter what I cooked, it wasn't as good as Tom's.

I always thought I knew how to cook. I found out later I really didn't, and I couldn't please Tom. So, I decided to go on strike and let Tom do the cooking. To my surprise, Tom was an excellent cook. He learned a lot of recipes from cooks on the boats he ran while commercial fishing. Since then, I began to learn how to cook. If I got stumped, I would call Tom's mom and ask her how to fix it.

When it came time to plan meals for the lodge, I searched for the easiest and best recipes I could find. I had help from our neighbors on how to plan and what to serve. They were a big help.

After searching through dozens of recipes, I found an excellent rec-ipe for seafood fettuccine. It became one of our most popular meals. The easiest first-class recipes were caught out of our front yard—baked halibut, sautéed salmon, and seafood fettuccine. We also did a delicious creole tomato and prawn sauté served over rice. We hired a man named Jerry to help with all aspects of the lodge. He was a persistent 17-year-old neighbor who enjoyed working in the kitchen and was eager to learn. He added his favorite Jerry's cheesecake to the menu. At the end of the season, Jerry left to attend college in Fairbanks, Alaska.

GETTING GROCERIES IN RURAL ALASKA

March 16th, 1995

I was able to get our grocery list faxed to Super Value in Ketchikan for our seasonal supply of meals—at least most of them. This was difficult for me since I had not planned on doing the cooking. I also didn't have any cooking experience. Our groceries were to be flown out with the mail the next day, weather permitting.

I soon began ordering groceries for the next groups that I could put on the float plane while the current guests came in. I had to plan ahead, especially for the produce.

MEAL PLAN AND RECIPES

Prince of Wales Island, Alaska.

MEAL MENU

FEATURING HOME
BAKED DESERTS
AND LOCAL
CUISINE IN A FIRST
CLASS.
FULL SERVICE
LODGE .

THANK YOU FOR DINING WITH US

DAY 1

BREAKFAST
CINNAMON FRENCH TOAST ,BACON/
SAUSAGE,FRESH FRUIT,EGGS TO ORDER.
ALL BREAKFAST
INCLUDE:COFFEE,TEA,COCOA,MILK,ORANGE JUICE.
CEREAL AND OATMEAL AVAILABLE ON REQUEST!

APPETIZER
WELCOME SALMON LOG

DINNER
GRILLED ALASKAN SALMON
STEAKS,BAKED POTATOES,STEAMED
BROCCOLI W/ FRESH HERB SEASONING,
FRESH BAKED BREAD,GREEK SALAD.

DESSERT
HOME BAKED APPLE PIE
AND/OR BLUEBERRY DELIGHT.

SPECIAL ATTENTION TO
DIETARY NEEDS!

LUNCH
SANDWICHES:
DELI HAM,TURKEY,SALMON AND
HALIBUT SPREAD.
FRESH FRUIT,
HOMEMADE COOKIES (CHOCOLATE CHIP,
PEANUT BUTTER,BRAN RAISIN OATMEAL.)
POP,COFFEE.

DAY 2

BREAKFAST
HOME FRIED POTATOES,BACON/SAUSAGE,
EGGS TO ORDER, MUFFINS, FRESH FRUIT.

APPETIZER
SALMON PATTIES,GARLIC SPICED SAUCE.

DINNER
LONDON BROIL,MUSHROOMS,WHITE RICE,
VEGETABLE MEDLEY,FRESH WHITE
ROLLS,GARDEN SALAD.

DESSERT
FUDGE CAKE W/BUTTERCREAM FROSTING
AND/OR PEACH COBBLER.

DAY 3

BREAKFAST
SHRIMP BENEDICT, FRESH FRUIT

APPETIZER
SALMON OR CHICKEN QUESADILLA,SALSA

DINNER
BAKED HALIBUT ,BABY RED
POTATOES W/HERB BUTTER SEASONING,GLAZED
BABY CARROTS,JALAPENO CHEDDAR CORN
MUFFINS,WILTED SALAD.

DESSERT
BAILEY CHEESE CAKE AND/OR FRESH
APPLE CRISP.

DAY 4

BREAKFAST
BLUEBERRY PANCAKES,BACON/
SAUSAGE,EGGS TO ORDER,FRESH FRUIT.

APPETIZER
CLAM FRITTERS w/LIME TARTAR SAUCE.

DINNER
CHICKEN CORDON BLEU,RICE
PILAF,ASPARAGUS W/HOLLANDAISE
SAUCE,ROSEMARY BISCUITS,
FRESH GARDEN SALAD.

DESSERT
PINEAPPLE UPSIDE DOWN CAKE AND/OR
PEANUT BUTTER PIE.

DAY 5

BREAKFAST
SALMON AND SAUSAGE QUICHE,MUFFINS,
FRESH FRUIT PLATTER.

APPETIZER
SMOKED SALMON W/CRACKERS.

DINNER
SEAFOOD FETTUCCINE,GARLIC
BREAD,CAESAR SALAD.

DESSERT
CHERRIE CRUMB CAKE,SWEET ENGLISH
CUSTARD OVER BLUEBERRIES.

Bread Bowl / Desert

Day One   Served 12:00P.M.

Lunch

Clam Chowder
Salmon Log
Rolls
Cookies

Dinner

Meat: Sauteed Salmon Steaks and Baron of beef.
Vegetables : Steamed brocolli with cream cheese sauc
Red baby potatoes,boiled,with butter parsely.
Green Salad.
Warm rolls
Carrot cake and Pumpkin pie.
Compementary Wine
Coffee, Tea,Milk,Pop.

Day Two   *Eggs Benedict*   Breakfast   *Muffins*   Served 6:00A.M.

Fried potatoes
Sausage patties
Scrambled eggs
Toast
Fruit (Fresh Canalope, Honey dew, apples, oranges,bannanas,) Cottage cheese and peaches
Cereal (Granola with cinnomon, honey. Raisin bran, Special K.)
Juice (Orange, Apple.)
Coffee,Tea, Milk.

Lunch   Served on the boat

Turkey sandwiches,Two per person. White or Wheat bread.
Lettuce,Tomatoe on the side.
Apple
Chocolate chip cookies, Six per person.
Coffee,Tea, Pop.

Dinner   *chicken Fettuccini*   Served 6:00P.M.

Seafood fettuccini and ~~Beef Stroganoff~~.
Ceaser salad
Sliced warm bread
Pumpkin pie and Carrot Cake.
Complimentary wine

Day Three   *Muffins*   Breakfast   Served 6:00 A.M.

Blueberry pancakes
Scrambled eggs
Bacon
Fresh Fruit   (Cottage cheese and peaches.)Canalope, Honey dew, bannanas, apples.)
Cereal
Juice (Apple, Orange)
Coffee,Tea,Milk.

Lunch   Served on the boat.

Ham Sandwiches.Two per person.White or Wheat bread.
Lettuce and Tomatoe on the side.
Apple
Peanut butter cookies.Six per person.
Coffee, Tea, Pop.

Dinner   Served 6:00P.M.

Baked Halibut and Pork Loin Roast .
Baby red potatoes with butter parsely.
Baby carrots
Green Salad
Rolls
Apple pie.
Complimentary wine.

Day Four   Breakfast   Served 6:00 A.M.

Hashbrowns   *muffins*
Scrambled eggs
Sausage
Fresh fruit (Canalope,Honey dew,Apple,Bannanas)
Cereal
Juice (Apple,Orange)
Coffee,Tea, Milk
Toast

Lunch   Served on the boat

Turkey sandwiches,Two per person.
Lettuce and Tomatoes on the side.
Apple
Chocolate chip cookies, Six per person.
Coffee,Tea,Pop

Dinner   *grilled*   Served 6:00 P.M.
                      Chicken breasts.
B.B.Q. Salmon and B.B.Q. ~~Boneless country pork ribs~~.
Potatoe salad
Baked beans
Rolls
Corn on the cob when in season.
Jacobs cheese cake.
Complimentary wine
Coffee,Tea,Milk.

Day Five   Breakfast   served 6:00

French Toast
Scrambled eggs
Bacon
Fresh Fruit (Canalope,Honey dew,Apple,Bannanas.)Cottage cheese and peaches.
Juice (Orange,Apple.)
Coffee,Tea, Milk.
Cereal

Lunch   Served 1:00

Prawn Tomatoe,onion,stir fry
Rice
Green Salad
Warm Bread   *crumb*
Cherrie,Pineapple,dump cake.

RECIPES

BAKED HALIBUT

(Serves 4-6)

4 halibut fillets (each, 6-8 oz. or ½ lb. each)
4 tablespoons mayonnaise
1 teaspoon Johnny's Seasoning Salt

Place fillets in baking dish. Spread light layer of mayonnaise over the top of each fillet. Too much mayonnaise will ruin the flavor of the dish. Sprinkle with Johnny's Seasoning Salt. Bake in 350-degree oven for approximately 20-30 minutes. Do not overcook.

PORK LOIN ROAST

(Serves 8)

1 (3 pound) pork loin
Garlic powder (or fresh garlic, sliced)
Salt, to taste
Fresh ground pepper, to taste
1 tablespoon olive oil

Poke small holes in top of roast. Season top of roast with salt, pepper, garlic powder (if using fresh sliced garlic, insert into holes in top of the roast). Coat roast with olive oil. Cover and bake in 350-degree oven for one hour. Remove covering and bake until meat thermometer reads well done (160 degrees). Let rest for 10 minutes; slice and serve warm.

BARON OF BEEF (TOP ROUND)

(Serves 8)

1 (3 pound) beef top round roast
Garlic powder, to taste
Salt, to taste
Pepper, to taste
1 ½ tablespoons, olive oil

Poke small holes in top of roast. Season with salt, pepper, garlic powder. Coat top of roast with olive oil. Bake uncovered in 350-degree
oven until meat thermometer reads medium well (150 degrees). Let
rest for 10 minutes; slice and serve warm.

BOSTON CLAM CHOWDER

(Serves 3-5)

½ cup celery, chopped
1 medium white or yellow onion, chopped
4 medium-sized potatoes, cubed
2 strips of bacon, finely chopped and lightly browned
3 tablespoons parsley, chopped
¾ cup butter, cubed
½ teaspoon pepper
½ cup water
Salt to taste
Fresh ground black pepper to taste
2 cups of milk
3 (6 ounce) cans of clams

Placed finely chopped bacon in a large stockpot over medium heat;
cook and stir until nearly crisp. Place onions and celery in a skillet;
cook until soft, about 5 minutes. Stir in ½ cup water and potatoes, season with salt and pepper; let simmer for 15 minutes, until potatoes are
tender. Add two cups milk and turn to low temperature. Stir for a few
minutes without boiling, then add butter and chopped parsley and
clams. Continue to stir occasionally for about 5 minutes. Let stand for
one hour, then reheat. *(For 5 or more, double recipe)*

SEAFOOD FETTUCCINE

(Serves 8)

1 ½ tablespoons butter
2 cloves garlic
¼ pound mushrooms
12 prawns
1 pound halibut, cut into cubes
1 cup grated parmesan cheese
1 cup heavy cream (or milk)

1 cup sour cream
2 tablespoons parsley
Vermouth, a splash if desired

Sauté garlic, butter, seafood, and mushrooms until cooked through. In large pot, mix in heavy cream, parmesan cheese, and sour cream. Add sauté mixture to pot and mix. Add parsley. Cook on stovetop at low to medium temperature. Serve on top of 16 ounces of cooked fettucine noodles.

DAD'S SMOKED SALMON

10 pounds salmon

For the brine:
1 cup rock salt
1 gallon water
2 cups dark brown sugar
1 teaspoon garlic juice

For the brine, make sure rock salt is dissolved into boiling gallon of water before adding brown sugar, let dissolve. Let brine mixture sit for 2-4 hours.

Add salmon to the brine mixture in glass (or plastic, if needed; do not place in metal). Let salmon sit in brine for 8-36 hours and no more or else it will be too salty. Remove salmon from brine, rinse briefly under cold running water, then pat dry. Set salmon on bottom rack of the oven and let sit overnight.

TARTAR SAUCE

2 cups mayonnaise
2 pickles, grated

Mix all ingredients in a small bowl.

CAESAR SALAD DRESSING

1 cup olive oil
1 cup red wine vinegar
4 cloves fresh garlic, diced or grated

1 teaspoon salt
1 teaspoon pepper

Mix all ingredients in a small bowl till combined.

TOMATO AND PRAWN STIR FRY

(Serves 4)

1 pound prawns or shrimp, peeled and deveined
2 tomatoes, blanched
4 green onions, large chopped
3 cloves garlic, diced
¼ cup butter

In a skillet, sauté garlic and prawns over medium-high heat; add green onions and tomatoes. Mix well and serve over rice.

SHRIMP CREOLE

(Serves 4)

1 ½ pound prawns or shrimp, peeled and deveined
Green onions, chopped
Mushrooms, chopped
2 cloves garlic, finely chopped
1 cup red wine
Tony Chachere's Creole Seasoning
1 red pepper - seeds and membrane removed, finely chopped
1 green pepper - seeds and membrane removed, finely chopped
1 can (14.5 ounce) stewed tomatoes
2 cans (14.5 ounce) tomato sauce

In a small pot or large skillet, cook red pepper, green pepper, and garlic in 1 cup red wine, let reduce on low heat for 10 minutes. Add mushrooms, tomato sauce, and stewed tomatoes and their juices, and bring heat up to medium. Add 1 teaspoon of Tony Chachere's to the mix and stir in; let mixture simmer for 5-10 minutes. Add shrimp and cook for 1-2 minutes until firm, flip and cook for another 1-2 minutes. Take off heat; add in green onions as well as salt, pepper, and Tony Chachere's to taste.

SALMON PATTIES

(Serves 4)

1 (16 ounce) jar salmon
½ onion, chopped fine
2 tablespoons mayonnaise
2 medium potatoes, diced and boiled
½ teaspoon dillweed
2 eggs

Mix all ingredients in a small bowl and form into patties. Brown in a small amount of oil.

Poor Man's Lobster

(Serves 4-6)

1 gallon water
1 cup sugar
Dash of salt
2 pounds halibut

Bring water to a boil. Add halibut. When halibut floats, fish is done. Take out. Serve with melted butter or tartar sauce.

Caesar Salad

(Serves 4 as a side)

1 head romaine lettuce
1/3 cup grated parmesan cheese
Salt to taste
Pepper to taste
1 lemon
Caesar dressing (see our Caesar dressing recipe)

Rinse, dry, chop (or tear) romaine in bite-sized pieces into individual bowls or one large bowl. Add light coating of Caesar dressing. Sprinkle with parmesan. Season with salt and pepper to taste. Squeeze lemon over top and serve immediately.

CHAPTER 9

SALTWATER PLAYTIME

March 26th, 1995

Tom, Jerry (our lodge assistant), and I went fishing in the new Osprey boat for the first time since we got it.

We caught 12 bottom fish and no salmon. The weather was beautiful. It was in the 50s. After Tom and Jerry cleaned and fileted the fish, they gave the carcasses to our neighbors to feed the minks hanging around under their dock.

April 3rd, 1995

Tom and I went fishing on Sunday and caught a 20 lb. king right in front of our property. It was incredible.

Everyone in the bay was watching me fight the fish. We shared it with our neighbors. Tom said, "You are supposed to give away your first fish of the year for good luck."

Saturday, we had Jerry's parents and his sister over for dinner. We did this, in part, to help Jerry and I get used to working together, and so Jerry could get familiar with the kitchen.

"I think I'm going to enjoy this business. Even if I have to cook," I said.

That night, I asked Tom to help with the dishes. We all made a good team.

A funny thing happened the other night. We woke up to a woodpecker pecking on the side of the lodge. I didn't know there were woodpeckers in Alaska.

CHAPTER 10

FIRST PAYING GUESTS

April 18th, 1995

W e had our first paying guest stay for six nights. She is the local EMT instructor and was in class all week. Tom and I were supposed to take the whole class, but we only finished the CPR portion. We had too much work to complete at the lodge to concentrate.

I made sure there was sliced roast beef and turkey for sandwiches. I made a double batch of cookie dough and extra biscuits ahead of time. Jerry helped set the table. Tonight, I had Jerry make apple crisps for dessert. He did the dishes and left around 9 p.m.

I felt a little stressed occasionally, but with Jerry's help, I knew I would do just fine.

Everything went well. The first night, I had a slight problem. I was roasting a chuck roast when the propane ran out. Tom was out fishing. I called my neighbors and asked them to get Tom on the radio to come in and change the propane tanks because I didn't know how to. Dinner was an hour late, but at least I didn't panic.

I soon began making homemade buns and bread. I also sliced turkey and roast beef and froze it to keep. As I got more confident with my kitchen skills, for lunch, I would make homemade sourdough bread and use it to make turkey or roast beef sandwiches, and chocolate chip and peanut butter cookies. I was able to get sourdough starter from my neighbor. Our clients loved the homemade cookies.

FIRST FULL-SERVICE GUESTS

April 22nd, 1995

We began preparing for our first full-service fishing guests. I had Jerry practice making cookies. I also taught him how to clean the bathroom and showed him where everything was located.

Tom has completed the dock so that the pilot from Ketchikan Air could bring our guests right to our dock. That was a major accomplishment.

My hands were terribly sore from yard work, hauling wood, and other manual labor that had to be done around the lodge. I had several cuts on my hands from rocks. I don't think I had ever been so rough with my hands before.

I was excited to see our first guests.

I felt like we were well prepared, even though we didn't get everything we wanted done.

Tom took a quick trip to town on the boat. He invited Marla O'Rusty, an older lady in the community to come along. When he got home, he told me she wouldn't use the toilet on the boat. He didn't know why. Marla O'Rusty lived by herself in a cabin on the boardwalk. She made her own whiskey and always had a flask in her back pocket. Tom woke up to a loud thump. To relieve herself, Marla had tried to use a rubber bucket on the deck, but it collapsed. Thankfully, she was fine.

April 29th, 1995

This last week while our guests were here, we had lows in the 60s and highs in the 70s. It was beautiful.

With our first guest, we caught a 20 lb. king and later, we caught a 25 lb. king. They didn't have much luck with halibut, but they did catch a nice lingcod.

I served fish and crab the whole time they were here. They would put crab pots out in the morning, then retrieve them on their way back to the lodge after fishing. So, we had fresh crab.

Tom and I enjoyed their company, but we were exhausted by the end of the week.

CHAPTER 11

TAKING A BREAK

Today, we took the day off and went to the road system to check out the creeks, which were wonderful and beautiful. We saw two deer and a black bear. The gorgeous black bear ran off the road but didn't appear to be afraid of us. Tom honked the horn and yelled to see what the bear would do. It just kept eating his berries. That was the closest I had ever seen a bear in the wild.

Tom took a detour down a lonely road off the main logging road. "Where are you going?" I asked.

"You will see," he said.

At the end of the road, Tom stopped the truck, pulled out a blanket, laid it on the ground, and had me join him for a romantic moment. Once we were finished, Tom mentioned a mosquito had bitten him on his butt.

Later, we went to a birthday party in the back bay on the beach. We got a good idea for a BBQ pit. It was a great day.

May 8th, 1995

This week, an old neighbor gave Tom some good tips on saltwater sport fishing. They caught their limit of king salmon, and Tom caught a 42-pounder, which was the biggest.

I even went out one day to fish, but it was too much for me to balance cooking and fishing in a single day. We had a successful week.

May 15th, 1995

We finally got the beach house finished enough to move in before our guests arrived on the 18th. We still had the extra room and the storage area to paint, as well as the exterior. Tom worked on getting our sign up on the dock this evening.

We got a call tonight from our first guests. They were ready to return with three other people at the end of May.

May 22nd, 1995

For the last five days, we had my brother and his clients stay at the lodge. This was the first time we needed Jerry to work with us, preparing food and handling fish. Everything went well. I received nice compliments on the meals and fresh cookies. Everyone wanted the recipes.

Tom found a great fishing hole, and they all fished to their limit in just four days.

June 28th, 1995

We had a group of four guests stay for four days and three nights. They were on weather hold in Ketchikan on their way out and had to stay the night there.

Once they got to the lodge and went out fishing, they had a fun time even though it rained the whole time during their stay.

They had to stay an extra night at the lodge because of the weather. They didn't mind at all. We gave them a $600 credit for the inconvenience. For dinner, we had BBQ chicken, potatoes, salad, and homemade rolls. They all asked for copies of the recipes and went home happy.

Last week, Tom and I went to explore the island. We stopped at El Captain to ask about cave tours and to check out some creeks along the drive to Craig, Alaska. We fished along the way. We caught six-inch cutthroat trout. I left our tackle box next to a creek. We didn't notice until it was too late to go back. We had an amazing trip. I wasn't impressed with Thorne Bay. I thought it was too industrial.

On the road, we ran into a couple who were checking out the island. They asked if we lost a tackle box. I couldn't believe they found it. It was my dad's. It had the name my dad called me when I was a child on top, "Pat Mae." I did not write it on there. I got very emotional thinking my dad was with me in spirit.

Coffman Cove was a nice community. We wanted to camp at Luck Lake sometime because it was so beautiful. There are all species of fish—steelhead, cutthroat trout, sockeye, and more. There is also a creek that runs into it.

We stopped in Thorne Bay to visit friends who live there. They have deer that visit daily. The deer played with our dog Coho, and I was able to get close enough to pet them.

CHAPTER 12

CATCHING FISH LIMITS

Our last group of four stayed for five days. On the first day, they caught their limit of fish. The limit was six salmon per person. The next day, they went freshwater fishing using flies and spinners, catching and releasing fish all day long.

This was the first group Tom took freshwater fishing. He felt confident that guests would be happy with the freshwater fishing.

The next day, they fished for salmon and halibut. They all limited out on halibut and were satisfied.

August was an exciting month. The whales fed just outside of our bay in large numbers. It was easy to see them come into the bay. They would surface when feeding on salmon. It was beautiful to see them breach—when the whale propels itself out of the water in either a spinning or non-spinning manner.

CHAPTER 13

WRAPPING UP FOR THE SEASON

September 24th, 1995

Tom and I wrapped up our 1995 season and were starting to think about the 1996 season. We needed 40 guests to break even. In 1995, we had 17 guests; Tom also had two charters from yachts that came into the bay. We had one bed-and-breakfast guest. Tom built a smoke-house. He kept busy smoking fish and hunting deer. I began picking berries for red huckleberry and blueberry jam. I learned the hard way not to soak the berries for too long in salt water. Blueberry pie becomes salt pie.

I also started getting our advertising set up for next year's bookings.

I felt more comfortable at the lodge now. I was not homesick any-more. Home wasn't the same anyway since I lost both my parents.

One of the minks made a home next to our dock in a hole at the bottom of a big tree. I watched them as they chased each other in and out of the hole and around the tree. It enjoyed treats of fish bones when Tom would get back from fishing. I hadn't seen an otter in a while. I hoped they would be back come winter.

October 1995

Tom and a friend went hunting for a deer. This was Tom's first time hunting deer in Alaska. He hunted ducks every year. Tom's friend was knowledgeable about hunting and butchering big game. I never liked the taste of venison. Growing up, I could not forget my mom sending us down to the canning room in the basement of our house to fetch some canned goods. We had concrete floors in the basement with a drain that the wash basin would run into. My dad hung his deer down there for several days. We were not aware Dad had the deer hanging down there. We would run into the deer when mom sent us to the basement to get something, and it scared us. The deer always had a gamey taste to it.

After three days of hunting, Tom and his friend came home with a small buck. Tom's friend showed Tom how to gut and butcher the deer before he went south. Tom took care of the deer at the neighbors' house, then brought home our share. I didn't have to worry about running into it hanging.

I was about to try my first Alaskan venison. "You shot it," I told Tom, "You have to cook it."

He took what he called the back strap and made steaks for dinner with fried potatoes, onions, and corn. I was hesitant to even try it. Tom swore I would love it. He was right. It was the best steak I had ever tasted—no gamey flavor at all.

We didn't serve venison to our guests.

After a few days, Tom took a roast out for me to cook. I had never cooked venison before. I remembered the way my mom would wrap the meat with bacon and roast it somehow. So, I used that recipe, and it turned out great. I even had enough drippings to make gravy. This was the best roast I had ever cooked. I served it with mashed potatoes, gravy, and steamed broccoli.

I called my neighbor to ask her how she cooked a venison roast. She asked me what part it was. I had no idea. Tom didn't tell me. He had gone hunting again. I was on my own.

CHAPTER 14

CABIN FEVER IS REAL

After staying at the lodge during the first winter, I found out that cabin fever was a real thing. When you can't get out of the village to go anywhere because the weather is so bad that the float planes can't make it in, and the water is too rough to take the boat to town, you feel stuck. Depression set in, and I thought I was going crazy. After this, we decided to stay in Washington for a few months while we did sport shows and promoted the lodge.

We rented a garage from a friend of my family. We made a bed on the ground and got by with minimum living quarters.

Our friend's daughter gave us handmade ornaments to hang on our small Christmas tree.

I needed to get a job to help with expenses. Times were tough. We made enough with the lodge to get us to the next season. However, it wasn't enough to get the extra things we needed. Eventually, Tom had to sell his halibut shares. He didn't plan on commercial halibut fishing any longer anyway.

I was able to get a job at Fred Meyer in Shoreline, Washington while we were in Washington to help with expenses.

January 15th, 1996

Tom and I just got back from attending the Portland Sportsmen's Exhibition. We spent five weeks in the Seattle area. We were a little disappointed that we did not get one booking at the show. We talked to other lodges like ours; they said we shouldn't be disappointed because we would get bookings after the show.

On the last day of the show, Tom and I were short with each other. It was an emotional experience. Thankfully, we got a lot of positive comments and several names and numbers for our mailing list.

The next week, we got a call from a prospective guest that wanted to book three to five people. I began working on phone calls and thank you notes to follow up with for our mailing list.

For the next couple of years, we stayed busy doing all we could to promote the lodge and keep the bookings coming. It was an interesting adventure. Fortunately, we had repeat clients. I was glad that the lodge was picking up. But I was exhausted and burnt out.

CHAPTER 15

FEELING CONFINED

September 7ᵗʰ, 1997

As time went by, I found myself to be too confined to the lodge. We had just completed our third season, and although the business and financial burden had been easier, the conscious thought of nothing but fishing and business had placed a burden on my relationship with Tom. I was feeling trapped. The plan we had was not working out for us. I felt more like an employee than a wife. If things didn't go right, Tom would get into a rage. At one point, he flipped the burn barrel upside down. This is a big oil drum we used as a burn barrel. This had me concerned about what could happen if he got upset again. When I asked him about it, he said he would never hurt me. Don't get me wrong, we still loved each other very much.

For the past few years, we had wanted a child. But we could not have a child without adoption or IVF. We thought when we purchased the lodge, we would be able to be together, raise our family, and enjoy what we were doing at the same time.

It had been three years, and we still weren't able to have a child. We weren't enjoying our situation.

I felt that having a child would make our lives complete. I'm not sure Tom felt the same. He said he would have liked to have a daughter. That made me think we were both on the same page.

I was at the lodge 24/7 while Tom was out fishing. We found ourselves doing the job of three people each.

We couldn't afford to hire any more help. We needed more bookings first. Even if we got more bookings there were a lot of additions and repairs, not to mention purchasing another boat. We needed these things to get the lodge to its fullest potential of eight guests. Two boats, and four guests per boat.

If we held on to it, we would not be able to get it to its fullest capacity without continuing to go further into debt. By that time, it would be too late for our goals.

We had to make a difficult decision, one of the hardest we ever had to make. We had to make our own lives a priority.

We decided to take the equity we had in the lodge and buy a house in Washington, then invest the rest in income-producing properties. Tom would continue doing what he loved best—fishing.

We hoped and believed the lodge would grow and that we'd enjoy watching it do so, knowing we built it from our hearts and souls. But at this point, we just wanted to sell.

No matter how hard we tried with the lodge, we just couldn't get ahead. I was shuffling money from one account to another to try to make ends meet.

We had a buyer interested, but they wouldn't make an offer—they only wanted to trade property. We were not interested in trading.

We packed all our personal belongings to take to Washington in case we got a sale.

At the end of the season, we had a client agree to help us out and paid for two weeks exclusively. They paid up front. This gave us the incentive to continue.

I read a quote that said, "We seem to focus so much on how we are going to fail that we forget how to make the business work for us so we can succeed."

Once we changed our focus, the bookings started coming in. Thankfully, we doubled last year's bookings.

CHAPTER 16

HIRING A COOK AND GUIDE

June 11ᵗʰ, 2000

We hired a guide from Minnesota who seemed to be working out well. The chef we hired, Chef Roger, he called himself, was ideal for the lodge.

One week after working for us, Chef Roger broke out with gout in his leg. He had to go back to Florida.

Just before a full house, I, Chef Patty, had to take over and do the cooking. It is amazing what you can do when you have no choice.

Everything was working out perfectly. However, for me to hire a chef in the middle of the season was next to impossible.

We were two weeks away from our busiest time, and I hadn't had one qualified inquiry for the chef position.

I was so overwhelmed with everything, just trying to keep up. Thinking about the menu and if I could make it all flow was heavy on my mind. Booking new clients, taking deposits, sending receipts, paying bills, cleaning rooms every day, greeting the guests, entertaining the guests when they came in.

"I don't know how much more I can handle," I told Tom.

We had a couple make reservations because of the sales ads we had last year to sell the lodge. They had a wonderful time and said they would be very interested in making an offer. Tom wasn't excited at all. This made me feel guilty for trying to get the lodge sold. I told him the only thing I could think of would be a partnership situation. Tom could work as a guide, and the new owners could run the lodge. I was so upset I was making myself sick. This was ridiculous because we hadn't even seen the offer yet.

I decided I would wait until we saw a serious offer before I got myself so worked up. I was frustrated with our situation.

Daily, I was planning breakfast, lunch, and dinner not only for our guests but for our help. I would also clean both the beach house and the lodge, take reservations, send out invoices, and order groceries for the next group. I would follow up with the guests to make sure they were coming in on time, then would make homemade cookies, salad dressing, and bread, so I could prepare lunches for the next day.

I had to get our mailings out as soon as possible; advertising and our mailing list had to stay updated. I had a hard time remembering to follow up, which was most important.

I burned out during this season. Not only did I work on the business but I also helped build our crew's quarters. We even added a new boat and ramp this season.

I was so into the business that I forgot to pay the mortgage on the lodge. I had to wire the payment. I never missed a payment in my life.

We had a father and son at the lodge. I picked some fresh blueberries to make a pie. My neighbor told me to soak the blueberries in case there were any worms. I soaked them overnight, then made the pie for dinner that night.

The son took a bite. I could tell something wasn't right. The dad said, "Eat it." I tried it to see what was going on. It tasted like salt. I didn't think to ask how long to soak the berries. My blueberry pie turned out to be a salt pie. I was so embarrassed. I brought out another dessert and told him he didn't have to eat the blueberry pie. Fortunately, I always had two desserts for the guests to choose from.

CHAPTER 17

PLANNING THE EXIT STRATEGY

August 30th, 2000

We finished our sixth season at the lodge.

We projected $100,000 in gross sales, but we did just under $120,000. We put the profit made back into the business. We had a new aluminum boat built and paid $40,000 for it. We had the same payment we had with our other boat. But this was a much nicer, dependable boat.

We also bought a new aluminum ramp. We put that on a lease payment.

Our problem—we were in the same financial situation as last year but with less debt owed.

We would have to borrow to get through the winter. I was determined to find a job in Bellingham so we could afford to buy a house to call home. I would use my real estate commission and what we had coming from the lot we sold in Pt. Baker to make the down payment.

We wouldn't open the lodge again until June 1, 2001.

Before I left to go to Bellingham, Tom said he would look at any offers on the lodge.

I gave up trying to sell the lodge because Tom changed his mind every time someone was interested. It was very frustrating for me. I felt like I was failing Tom.

I was focusing on trying to make it work for both of us. I just wasn't sure it could work without me being there. I was also working on getting our debt down, but it was difficult with all the improvements that needed to be made. Every year, however, seemed to get easier.

Tom and I only had three days this year to fish for ourselves. We were busy all season. If we got the lodge booked more, we'd be able to hire more help. We should have been able to enjoy more fishing for ourselves at that time.

The area had been changing for the better. People were improving their homes and there was new demand for property in our area. I could see the potential for the business's future. They were considering a halibut quota for guides and outfitters as well as a moratorium on lodges, which could happen within the next couple of years.

If they put a moratorium on lodges, it should appreciate the value of the lodges that are part of the moratorium. Supply and demand.

The same goes for the halibut quota. That would limit the number of guides that could fish for halibut.

CHAPTER 18

TRUST THAT GUT FEELING

When I was packing this year to come south, I had a strange feeling that it would be the last time. I am not sure what came over me, but the feeling was strong. Tom stayed behind to close the lodge for winter. I went to Washington by myself. Tom would join me later.

Taking the ferry was like camping out. You sleep on the floor in sleeping bags unless you are lucky enough to be the first on the boat to get a chair to sleep in or if you pay for a cabin. There were movies to watch and the Forest Service provided educational seminars.

The ferry back to Bellingham was nice. I met so many nice people. I had my sleeping bag and pillow and slept in the viewing lounge. I was upstairs, which had the best views. There was an older man who was a Tlingit and Haida Indian. He said his grandfather created the town of Klawock and they came from Kui Island. According to the Central Council, there are over 30,000 Tlingit and Haida Indians worldwide.

This man followed me everywhere on the boat. When I went to eat, he showed up; when I sat in the hall away from everyone, he showed up and always sat with me to talk. He lived in Ferndale, Washington now and brought a neighbor to Alaska with him. His neighbor had

Parkinson's Disease and was missing a part of a lung. They were both very nice and seemed to have had a great time together in Alaska.

March 5, 2001

We had a buyer interested in the lodge. Tom met them in January at the lodge. They were managers of a lodge in Kenai, Alaska.

They had more information than we did on our own property as well as the dock permit. They made an offer, and we accepted.

We expected to close by March 1st, but it took longer because the buyer had to search for a loan. They had investors who didn't help them completely. It took a lot longer than expected to deal with the buyer. We had to agree on terms and the buyers got their loan approved, all as of last week. Now their attorney is working on the contract. We had to send a copy of the contract we had with the seller we bought the lodge from.

We had to get creative. We had the buyers assume the loan we had with the seller. It is difficult to get loans on property in remote Alaska. Lenders require foundations, road access, septic or sewer. That is what made it difficult for our buyers to get a loan. Thankfully, my real estate knowledge helped me be creative to finally get it sold.

On February 28th, 2001, at 10:55 a.m. we were in Seattle at our attorney's office on the 24th floor when Seattle had a 6.5 magnitude earthquake. Tom stood next to the window. I was under the table with the attorney and the gal taking our deposition. I told Tom he should have been with me under the table. If we were going to go, I wanted to be together. Tom said he was looking for a way out.

We were there because we had a guide at the lodge who claimed he hurt his leg while pushing the wheelbarrow full of wood up the hill and was suing for a knee replacement. He told us our cook and others that it was an old injury from when he was a lineman. So, we denied the claim and had to go through the court system to fight the claim. I didn't know how much more I could take. My nerves were truly being tested.

Sadly, he ended up winning the claim. They said it was because he reinjured his knee at the lodge.

I had a new goal. Buy a fixer-upper while looking for the property to buy and build a home for us. We would then invest in income-producing property.

We made an offer on a fixer-upper in Silver Beach in Bellingham. We had the inspection done.

We then needed to find a contractor who would provide us with an estimate of how much it would cost to do the structural work. We could do the rest.

I started a new job at Home Depot as a garden specialist. It was like when I worked at Ernst Hardware in 1980. However, Home Depot had more products and paid better—the benefits were also good. I worked for Sears for three months prior to Home Depot. I enjoyed the people and working at Home Depot better than Sears.

I helped contractors in the store and thought, "I hope I can invest in properties someday." You had to learn and work in each department to give coworkers breaks. I learned a lot.

CHAPTER 19

THE IN VITRO PROCESS

In December, Tom and I went through the in vitro fertilization process. After giving myself shots twice a day for 14 days, we were
told I wasn't producing enough eggs to continue with it. I was dev-
astated and felt like a failure.

When my niece found out, she offered to donate eggs so we could
continue. I was in tears. I couldn't believe she would go through that
for us. She would have had to go through the same process, and she
hates shots. I couldn't put her through that.

We couldn't commit financially or emotionally at the time. We had
too much on our plates.

Regarding our former lodge, the last thing we heard was that the new
buyers split up and had to let the lodge go. They had been trying for
years to get pregnant. The husband did the guiding. They hired a handyman to help with repairs at the lodge. The wife ended up pregnant.
When the baby was born the baby looked just like the handyman.

Tom went to Craig, Alaska to start a new guiding service. Craig is
located at the other end of the island. Tom had his guests stay at
Ruthann's Hotel and eat at their restaurant. All Tom had to do was

guide, clean the fish, and entertain. I was so sad to hear about the end of a beautiful lodge we built.

ABOUT THE AUTHOR

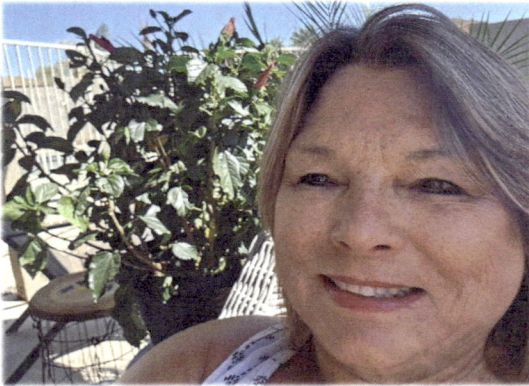

Patty Mae Gray was born and raised in Seattle, Washington. She grew up fishing, gardening, and investing in real estate.

In 1994, when Patty and her husband were moving to Port Protection, Alaska, she started her first journal. She is currently transforming her journals into novels.

She lives in Arizona with her dog, Lucy and parrot, Mattie.

Her goal is for her readers to enjoy and learn from each of her experiences through her stories.

Made in United States
Troutdale, OR
12/21/2024

27073435R00046